MOTHER, GOD, ME & THE WORLD

A COLLECTION OF 30 SHORT POEMS

SUGANDHA PALLAN

Copyright © Sugandha Pallan
All Rights Reserved.

This book has been published with all efforts taken to make the material error-free after the consent of the author. However, the author and the publisher do not assume and hereby disclaim any liability to any party for any loss, damage, or disruption caused by errors or omissions, whether such errors or omissions result from negligence, accident, or any other cause.

While every effort has been made to avoid any mistake or omission, this publication is being sold on the condition and understanding that neither the author nor the publishers or printers would be liable in any manner to any person by reason of any mistake or omission in this publication or for any action taken or omitted to be taken or advice rendered or accepted on the basis of this work. For any defect in printing or binding the publishers will be liable only to replace the defective copy by another copy of this work then available.

To family and friends,

To God,

To inner curiosity,

And to the readers.

Without you, it wouldn't be possible.

Contents

Preface .... *vii*

Mother

   1. You Can't Hold Me 3

   2. God Is Melting 4

   3. Stay With Me 5

   4. Oh! Mother 6

   5. I Oblige 7

   6. You Are Not Me 10

God

   7. Fearful 15

   8. Gift From Stranger 16

   9. Devil 17

   10. Goodbye God 18

   11. Embrace Me 19

   12. I See Now 20

Me

   13. What's With My Heart Today? 23

   14. Heart Is Awake 24

   15. Home 25

   16. I Stand At The Shore 26

   17. Emotion 27

   18. It Kills 28

   19. Let Me Write 29

   20. What If I Run Away? 32

Contents

21. Journey Of Life — 33

The World

22. When It Happens — 37
23. Dreams — 38
24. Unsaid — 39
25. The Screen — 40
26. Till Night Falls Again — 41
27. Poet Is Awake — 42
28. World Is Battling — 44
29. What It Takes? — 46
30. Senseless — 47

About The Author — 49

Preface

'Mother, God, Me & The World' is my first poetry book which is the collection of 30 poems in which I explore my relationship with Mother, God, myself and the relationship of human beings with the world, the four most important parts of our lives.

Well, chronologically, the book is divided into four parts 'Mother,' 'God,' 'Me,' and 'The World.' It is the same chronology in which a child sees things around him and understands as he grows older.

Part 1: Mother

The first person a child sees or gets to know immediately after taking birth is mother. The section consists of six poems in which I explore my relationship, our relationship with our mothers. From a foetus to an adult, as we grow older, this relationship changes. The section explores the feelings that a child goes through when he is small and fearful of his surroundings to when he grows old and then disappointments take over. The section ends with the end of this relationship.

Part 2: God

Before we can know ourselves, we know of that divine power watching over us. This relationship is also bitter-sweet or as it is said that no relationship is whole. The section contains six poems exploring our relationship with God. From disbelief to disappointment to final union, the poems explore them all.

Part 3: Me

Now we are old enough to know ourselves. There are nine poems in this section all exploring my or our relationship with ourselves. Being in my twenties, I explore the emotions and troubles that people of this age generally go through. Therefore, each of the poems might bring out different emotions in different readers with different life experiences.

Part 4: The World

Now is the moment of truth. This section talks about what's happening around and how human beings are related to each other. This section contains nine poems. Each poem talks about emotions that human beings generally go through.

So, in the book, I try to explore spirituality, human relationships as well as the relationship of people in a society in a writing style that may seem unique to many. Nevertheless, depth and meaning are what readers generally expect from a poet with various life experiences which urge readers to turn the pages and keep on turning them till they reach the last page. See what it means to you..

Mother

1. You can't hold me

I am water,
I will flow,
I am air,
I will blow,
I am sand,
I will slip away,
From your hand,
I am no spirit,
No flesh,
Or muscle mesh,
I am a rock,
with cracks,
With blood oozing out,
I am that blood,
Mother! You can't hold me.

2. God is melting

I am telling you
God is melting,
He melts when you don't go to Church,
And pray no more,
He melts when you don't sing hymns,
And light no candles,
He melts when you wander
Searching for me,
Oh mother, I am telling you
God is melting,
He will let me go.

3. Stay with me

Look!
In there!
There is someone
In my room,
He has no face,
Just two eyes,
Blood drips from them,
He doesn't speak,
But screams,
My ears are full of them,
Mother I fear him,
He fears you,
You knock,
He sneaks away,
Mother you leave,
He comes back,
Like cold winter,
He fears your warmth,
It burns him down,
Mother! Stay with me tonight.

4. Oh! Mother

Your curly locks, when touched your bosom,
You looked beautiful,
More beautiful than any princess can ever be,
You washed away that stain with so much ease,
Oh! Mother,
You have solution of every problem,
Don't you see something in my eyes?

5. I oblige

Dressed in black
You entered the room,
Like apocalypse,
Like impending doom,
But like beauty of birth,
Like springing bloom ,
Like utmost glee,
Like weary gloom,

Quiet were you
As you came close,
And I oblivious
To your purpose,
Were you here to bless
or to put a curse?
Your eyes were red
For you have wept,
For it troubled you
The secret you kept,

Now was the time
To reveal the truth,

*And I pondered
Like a sleuth,
I wondered what!
In my every thought,
About the beauty
Of the gift you brought,*

*Son! close your eyes
As you beseeched,
And more you cried
For the bond you breached,
Wrapped in red
You took the knife,
To stab my heart
To take my life,*

*You gifted me
Void in heart,
With every beat
I left a part,
You came closer
It drifted us apart,
Your beauty a murderer
Murder your art,*

*My last breath
Was your name,*

SUGANDHA PALLAN

My days were
Yours to claim,
You want my life
Then I may oblige,
The devil came
In mother's disguise.

6. You are not me

I look at you to find myself,
I look like you, they say,
They see your youth in me,
Maybe,
So, I look at you to find myself,
To see if I look like you as they say,
Your youth is long gone,
Your beauty is now perished,
Like a flower long dried,
I see your eyes,
They are often closed,
I look at you but you don't look,
Your mouth,
It is open unlike your eyes,
You have kept your teeth away,
Are you afraid you might die?
So, you don't eat anymore,
You have put away
Your body from your soul,
When I see your face,
Wrinkled forehead and cheeks,
You are meek and weak,

SUGANDHA PALLAN

Your thoughts bleak,
I wonder,
Do you have desires still?
Because memories have withered away,
Faded, shaded like old age,
Your hair is grey, silver sometimes,
But the braid is still long,
You nourish them with your beliefs,
Do you think still?
Because wit has withered away,
Cold, shivering like old age,
I look nothing like you, you look nothing like me,
But the comparison, scares me.

God

7. Fearful

He looked at me
From a distance,
From the crowd
That surrounded him,
His face smeared in blood,
His eyes fixated on me,
His clothes were tattered,
He looked battered,
When he cried,
Shed tears of blood,
He stood still,
Did nothing, said nothing,
They feared him,
He feared them,
I looked closely,
He was God,
The God feared men.

8. Gift from stranger

When he made me,
Filled my mind
With words,
My heart
With emotions,
Gifted me,
The unique art
Of poetry,
So, i write,
I sing,
I pray,
But i return
The gift today,
A gift from a stranger
Is not acceptable.

9. Devil

One day devil,
To test his evil,
Entered the human world,
He first broke silence,
Shattered the peace,
He then broke homes,
Ripped families apart,
He then parted lovers,
And broke the hearts,
But he couldn't match,
The evil of God,
For He broke trust.

10. Goodbye God

Goodbye God!
I bid you farewell
As I turn atheist,
Festivals will come and go,
Millions will rejoice,
I'll be submerged in my woes,
In Churches,
Hymns, the choirs will sing,
All will be same,
Just a voice will be missing,
The temples will see,
Impressions of thousand feet,
Grime will cover slowly,
The past impressions of only two feet,
Bon Voyage you say!
Bon Voyage I say!
Goodbye God,
I bid you farewell,
As I turn atheist.

11. Embrace me

Embrace me,
And take me in,
Show me,
The light within,
Wandering is enough to drain,
Running from you,
Hiding behind the pain,
In which, I was caught,
My sorrow, my fraught,
You touched me,
So tenderly,
Like you made me,
So slenderly,
I was a fool to not see,
Your love, that set me free,
Now I am here to pray,
Leaving behind distress and dismay,
So, God! Embrace me,
And take me in,
Show me,
The light within.

12. I see now

The rain has just stopped,
The sky is now clear,
The vision is not blocked,
Now I see clearly,
Your benevolence I didn't look,
Your kindness I overlooked before,
You sent the rain,
To wash away my pain,
It came with thunder,
To break the clutter,
And make the noise go away,
So, I hear you,
And you my soulful cries,

Me

13. What's with my heart today?

What's with my heart today?
It plunges,
And pounces,
And flutters,
And bounces,
It flies,
And dives,
And swims,
And sinks,
It rises,
And falls,
And runs,
And crawls,
It just fails to beat.

14. Heart is awake

Four walls,
With nothing inside,
Make sounds echo,
When on walls they glide,
The nights yawn,
In loneliness,
But the heart is awake,
in utter sleeplessness,
Bitter sweet memories,
when fade,
dissolving themselves,
In every shade,
My heart wakes,
with small desires,
with hopes and dreams,
That one aspires,
Four walls,
With nothing inside,
Make sounds echo,
When on walls they glide.

15. Home

Four walls surrounding me,
Where i struggle to breathe,
I used to call it home,
Two rooms fully furnished,
A roof covering my head,
Doors and windows partly opened,
There was a window,
Where mom and me sipped our tea,
That is the bed,
where she sang lullaby,
Memories are faded,
And i sit in a corner,
Here i struggle to breathe,
I used to call it home.

16. I stand at the shore

Waves of the ocean,
High as sky,
Great as god,
Devouring your waters,
Predator, killer, murderer,
Here I stand at the shore,
Cool breeze touches my bangs,
My cheeks go frozen,
My lips go blue,
My eyes go dry,
There is no end to this ocean,
The ocean so wide,
The ocean so deep,
Here you come another wave,
I brace myself,
Devour me, eat me, kill me,
I'll touch your bed,
And rise to the sky.

17. Emotion

Overwhelming me
What is this emotion?
Nowhere can I feel
My presence,
Not even
Inside me,
It is the emotion
That overshadows me,
My existence,
My identity,
My self.

18. It kills

Cut me into pieces
I won't cry,
Don't make me feel
useless,
It hurts,
Set me on fire
I won't scream,
Don't make me feel worthless
It burns,
Leave me in darkest forest
I won't be scared,
Don't make me feel alone
It scares,
Stab me with knives
I won't die,
Don't back stab me
It kills.

19. Let me write

It happens
All the time,
Whenever I try
To write,
I am taken away
To my distant memories,
To emotions unexplored,
To paths
I never tread,
There are distractions!
There are distractions
Around me,
That do not let me
Do what I strive for,
What I live for,
And what I write for,
The mind wanders
Like a vagabond,
It is not still,
It is not here,
It is somewhere
Distant,

Looking into
The distant memories,
I call you my heart,
I can you my mind,
Come back!
Here is your place,
It's here you belong,
Oh! My body,
Oh! My soul,
Why can't you just behold?
The mind that is far away,
Chain it up
To the walls inside,
Why can't you stop my mind?
From wandering,
Are you a nomad?
Are you a hipster?
What are you?
Who are you?
How dare you?
Just come here!
And let me write,
About the things,
That are not about you,
That do not please you,
That do not bother you,
But me,

SUGANDHA PALLAN

But us,
For once
Let me write,
Because it's not a fight,
It's a union,
You and me
Make us,
Oh! My mind,
For once
Let me write.

20. What if I run away?

What if I run away?
Leaving everything behind,
To a place unknown,
Known to no humankind,
Will I ever return?
Will I be forgiven?
When I take another birth
Will it be a reason for your mirth?
What if I take away?
The memories with me,
Will you still remember
Or your mind be free?
What if I run away?
Leaving everything behind
Will you be the same?
Or will you be kind?

21. Journey of life

On the road, in the car,
Driving for long, it was still so far,
Dark night, raining too,
I was afraid, what to do,
Solitary road, me too alone,
Frightened heart, in this lone,
I drove and drove, for very long,
To break the monotony, listened to a song,
After some miles, the rain stopped,
Clouds vanished, I hoped,
The time passed and passed through,
Showed me world's false and trues,
Then I saw a human again
it was a woman,
Carrying a baby, in her arms,
Walking slowly, beside the farms,
That beautiful lady was bare foot
I approached her, offered her my boot,
She refused though, called her life not worth a buck,
Unfortunately, it was her bad luck,
I started my odyssey once again,
I was fatigued, was in pain,

But the journey was momentous too,
Abstruse to decide, what to do,
Ultimately, I achieved my aim,
I got some fans and a lot of fame,
The journey of life is not easy,
Every day, every second is busy,
I gathered my memories together,
I kept them in heart forever,
My ashes blew, as I left the world,
But some of my questions are still unanswered.

The World

22. When it happens

When you fear a moment,
And it happens,
You realize
You didn't die,
You are
Breathing,
Your heart
Beating,
You realize
You are alive,
And living,
And that is how
You become more alive,
With every experience,
With every such moment,
You become more alive.

23. Dreams

If you love your dreams,
Even when they are broken,
In pieces so small,
That you can't count them all,
They will rise from their ashes,
Like Phoenix,
They will come to you,
Breaking all manacles,
Smashing all shackles,
To embrace you,
So, they grow like a tree,
You have to water them everyday,
They will come back one day,
If you love them truly,
They will rise from the dead.

24. Unsaid

We start with writing our names,
We end up writing our feelings,
Emotions that are not said,
Feelings that are unshared,
Concealed, hidden deep inside,
Then we tear the paper,
In pieces,
As our hearts,
Bits and pieces scattered everywhere,
The unsaid remains unsaid.

25. The screen

What are these sounds?
As someone chewing the flesh,
The cracking of bones,
The shattering of hopes,
See these people!
They have lost humanness,
Now engrossed in the screen,
A drool comes out of their mouth,
Their eyes wide open,
And darkness surrounding them,
They have lost something,
They have lost the dreams,
They see, they pray, they love the screen.

26. Till night falls again

And it will be morning in a while,
The sun is about to rise,
So, you breathe,
The memories won't haunt you,
You breathe,
The past won't taunt you,
And breathe the world is waking,
Breathe for the dawn is breaking,
You breathe,
For there is no sound,
And breathe,
For the sorrow won't hound,
You breathe,
There is no one around,
And breathe,
New desires are found,
You breathe,
Till it withers away the pain,
Oh! soul,
Breathe,
Till the night falls again.

27. Poet is awake

When the man dozes off to sleep,
The poet is awake,
Like time has stopped,
Like night never came,
Like sun is still up there,
Shining bright over heads,
So, you kill the man,
Put him to rest,
And the only one alive,
Is a poet with pen,
To pass the time's test,
Write whatever you like,
Seek the answers,
Deep hidden inside,
What is there in the world for me?
What do I seek?
What makes me long?
What makes me belong?
Woven in words the foreplay,
And then you act wise,
Oh! The words don't rhyme,
Don't worry,

SUGANDHA PALLAN

Not everything has to rhyme,
So, put away your fears,
Remembered are those,
Jarring to the ears.

28. World is battling

The world is battling,
It is surely battling,
The fight is not over,
It's far from over,

The struggles have come to light,
Those which were hidden inside,
The walls of heart and mind,
Concealed deep inside,

The mind has come forward,
The emotions have broken borders,
The layers are finally ripped apart,
And all of us playing our part,

The world is battling,
It's battling itself,
It's battling misery,
It's battling torture,
It's battling less,
When the less is more,

SUGANDHA PALLAN

The world is batting,
It's battling body,
It's battling soul,
It's battling outside,
And the inner sore,

The world is battling,
It's battling death,
It's battling despair,
It's battling for things,
That are beyond repair,

The world is battling,
It's far from over.

29. What it takes?

What it takes?
It takes blood from your body,
Skin from your bones,
Vision from your eyes,
When you give it your everything,
It takes your everything.

30. Senseless

These are just words,
They don't make sense,
Not everything
Has to make sense,
Sensible are those,
Who can be senseless as a child,
With naivete in genes,
And joy in mind,
The wisdom of sages,
Couldn't bring the joy,
Cheerful are those,
Who act without a ploy,
The words of wordsmiths,
Couldn't treat a sore,
Thoughtful are those,
Who look within for cure.

About The Author

Sugandha goes by her pen name Sugandha Pallan. Born in 1995 in Delhi, India, Sugandha was drawn to poetry from a very young age. She has been a student of literature and holds a Master's degree in English Literature. Sugandha has been a journalist before with experience in national dailies and national public service broadcaster of India.

www.ingramcontent.com/pod-product-compliance
Lightning Source LLC
LaVergne TN
LVHW041546060526
838200LV00037B/1160